The All-True, Secret Diary of an Ugly Break-Up

A novella by

Leanne Fullerton

About the cover and the Kintsugi heart

Kintsugi is the Japanese art of putting broken pieces back together with gold – built on the idea that, in embracing damage and inperfections, you can create something even stronger and more beautiful.

"There is a crack in everything – that's how the light gets in." – *Leonard Cohen*

For Michael

Table of Contents

Introduction

"Let's face it... he ain't a catch

He's a boy in a man's body
He's angry at the world
He complains all the time
He's impatient
He's messy
He's not affectionate
He doesn't kiss you for real
He doesn't ever make love
He doesn't make any effort with sex
He's pretty selfish
He makes you feel inadequate
He's quick to decide what's wrong with you
He doesn't value you

You have enough memories, you don't need more."

•••••••••••••

We were treasure hunting in one of the myriad thrift stores downtown. As Mike became entranced by some vintage bar signs, I wandered over and started poking through a box of books which was tucked under a card table. Beneath a few astute hardcovers and artsy books, was a rich vein of current fiction and non-fiction paperbacks. But it was the softcover leather book stuck in the mix, the one with no title on the spine, which I pulled from the box.

Flipping it open, I quickly realized this wasn't a book but a diary of some sorts – clearly written by someone who was going through something. It began with a laundry list of some man's shortcomings, and alluded to his having recently gone off with another woman. No wonder the diary's author was upset.

Did the person who penned these words know that their highly-personal journal had gotten thrown in with the other books? Have they noticed by now that it's gone? Are they horrified thinking that someone is reading their private words?

Mike was still caught up with inspecting a neon "Pabst Blue Ribbon" sign, so I settled myself onto a bench the back corner of the booth and kept reading. Maybe it was wrong, but I couldn't help it.

Mainly because I instantly understood this person. I had been her. And by the time Mike had decided against the sign – with no help from me, I might add – I knew I was taking this journal home with me. I had become protective of this poor, injured soul and her words. I wasn't going to give anyone a chance to casually glance over them and have a laugh.

And besides, I wanted to see how it turned out for her.

At home, with Mike busy watching his sports, I went upstairs and settled in a chair with the diary. It's hard to know if the big glass of Merlot was a good or a bad idea, but I was thankful to have it there to sip on as I turned the pages and discovered that a lot of her words cut very close to the bone.

How many of these same torturous, self-defeating, cyclical thoughts had I suffered through? The whys of what happened, and the self-esteem left in tatters. I found myself crying for her, and for me – specifically the me that had been through a devastating break-up nine years earlier that I thought I would never get over. Sharing her pain and her experience, strangely, helped me sort out and lay to rest some of my old baggage.

They say we all go through this stuff. But I didn't fully understand just how much our experiences are identical until I read the secret diary. It's why I feel compelled to share it now. I don't feel I am betraying the author because, 1) the diary offers no clues as to her identity and, 2) I have changed the names of everyone she mentions.

Hopefully this journal can do the same for anyone else going through an ugly break-up. It lets you know that you aren't alone, and that when someone tells you, "I understand. I've been there," they're telling you the truth.

February

February 2nd

Stuff I can't say to anyone:

I believed him when he said his former marriage had damaged him. He seemed damaged, but I told myself I could fix him. He didn't feel like he could ever love someone again, and he didn't think he wanted to try. He was afraid. I reassured him, and I reassured myself. I had enough love for both of us. I was strong enough for both of us. I could definitely fix him.

And he let me stay. For six years.

Six years when he really didn't care that much about me. I was handy to have around, convenient. I adored him, would do anything for him. Let him set the parameters. Because I knew my loving care could heal his heart.

What can I say? I was young (but, shamefully, not that young). And I was really, really stupid.

He had issues with his parents, and with work. I was there for him to lean on, the complete, consummate friend. He went through some rough times, and I was there to see him through them, help him through them. And then finally the pieces of his life started coming together, and he rebuilt himself. Now here he is, ready to start a whole new happy life. And he's choosing for that life to be with someone who is not me.

He's gone and left me for dead.

How did I get here? What could I have done to stop my life from turning to crap?

I can't possibly share this with my girlfriends. They've never thought much of him, and I just can't handle their disgust of him right now. I don't mind the "I told you so"s as much as I do having to break down and analyze just how horrible he was, in gruesome detail.

So I'm saying all the ugly stuff here. The selfish, petty, immature, wounded, self-pitying stuff that I don't dare show the world. To them I want to appear as if it's simply a love affair which ran its course, we wanted different things, went our separate ways, and all that civilized stuff.

But the truth is, I'm a wreck. A weeping, damaged wreck. So messed up that I bought a book on how to handle break-ups, just to know I'm not alone. It suggested I start a journal to say everything that no one else wants to hear. So here we are.

In fact, one of the writers of the break-up book talked about everything he did to get over a break-up, saying he "journaled, collaged and decoupaged." Wrote letters to his anger, built a voodoo doll of his fears and created a dance to celebrate his uniqueness. And jokingly suggested making a papier-mache hat of your dreams.

Don't think I will be doing any of the rest of that stuff, but I'm grateful for the journal idea.

I apologize in advance for all of the bad thoughts and energy I'm about to put into you.

February 3rd

I'm feeling angry today.

I didn't think I'd be feeling anger at this point. I really thought the worst feelings were over. I guess it was a stage I'd either skipped or hadn't gotten to yet.

What are those stages of grief again?

Denial, anger, bargaining, depression, acceptance.

Crap.

I'm only on Stage 2.

But I'm feeling like a world-class chump. And he's a world-class asshole.

Part of me wants to confront him, rip him to shreds. But silence is my only power.

Besides, he's such a jerk that reason and understanding will never get through. He's too self-absorbed, too full of himself, too full of shit. But I digress.

I feel used, but as much as I want to denounce him for all his many transgressions, I want to come out of this with some dignity.

Silence gives me dignity, class, power and sanity. 'Cause the truth is, silence is my only protection from pain. Communicating with him is inviting back into my life a person who is all-too-willing to inflict heartache.

And a lot of what I want to say, I don't have the strength or the stomach to say. To speak out loud some of the things I think would most likely finish me off.

As much as I wish for the big, "Sorry, you mean the world to me" call or letter, I really hope I never speak to him again. If it is by any means within my power, then I intend to make sure that's so.

February 9th

Only my pride wants him to take back his choice.

The rest of me wants a new life, a clean slate, filled with potential suitors who will be so much better than him.

The next man in my life will be:

Loving and affectionate
Adoring
Strong yet gentle
Grounded, sensible
Happy (or at least content)
Thoughtful
Supportive and loyal
Kind and faithful
Funny and fun to be with

He'll think I'm the most amazing woman and cannot believe his luck that he got me to fall for him. He'll be so in love with me that he can't keep his hands off me. He'll think I'm so perfect that he won't be interested in other women. He will be a great lover, and a faithful one. I'll never have to be suspicious and he'll never give me reason to be. I will be able to trust him on every level.

He will not only love and adore me, but respect and like me as well. He will admire my good qualities and be understanding of my bad ones.

And he will be worthy of all the love I give him.

He will deserve to have me.

I will never, ever again settle for so little. I'd be better off alone. I will hold out for this new guy.

February 12th

A lovely day at the beach. 70s and sunny. Lunch by the ocean. Everything to lift one's spirits, and I'm glad of it because I've been backsliding.

I'm having anger, but I also wonder way too much if he is thinking of me and missing me, and feeling any sort of remorse for his behavior or for losing me.

I think of things I want to say to him, but they will never bring him to regret or change his course, or own up to his actions. By now in his mind, I left him for someone else.

I hate that he feels he owes me nothing.

I hate that he's getting on with his new woman, completely unfettered, without tiresome me to contend with.

I hate that he doesn't really care about me.

And I hate that it's almost Valentine's Day, a.k.a. SAD ("Singles Awareness Day"). Too depressing to discuss. Let's just try to pretend it's not happening and get through those awful twenty-four hours.

February 19th

I really should write about the good days, the painless days, so I'm reminded that generally I'm doing okay, when a "back-up" day comes. Like today.

So he called me last Friday for my address (?!?) and we talked for about half an hour, much longer than we should have. Nothing but chitchat. I finally made noises like I was holding back tears and he happily hurried off the phone.

I hope he worries about me and feels crappy about me, but I think it's a vain hope. The person who does the dumping always seems to move on with the greatest of ease.

My best strategy is to say nothing accusatory and let him feel shitty about the pain I'm trying to cover. Yes, this is where I am, still stuck in "What is he thinking?"

I guess he was glad to talk to me, and I'm glad he's the one doing the contacting. I hope that chat made him miss me. I guess I want him to hurt as much as I'm hurting. It's probably not possible, but I can still wish for it.

See, I'm in a bad way today. A few possible reasons:

1) PMS.
2) Yesterday I finally notified everyone of the break-up and it stirred up all the ugliness. Even with keeping it brief, I still found it painful.
3) The phone convo, which definitely sent me into a tailspin.
4) Having to use the apartment building's laundry instead of doing it at his place (for some reason, this really upset me today, probably because I'm getting low on quarters).

Whatever the reason(s), I'm very weepy this afternoon. I had stopped crying over him, and now I'm back at it. I told everyone I'm doing well, and now I'm feeling like I did five weeks ago, like I've barely made any progress.

Last night I flipped through the break-ups book, and came away thinking I've moved on from the place they're describing.

But today I've got Kleenex with me at all times. What is going on?!

Last week I never wanted to speak to him again. This week I want to say stuff to him. Good and bad things. It's the first time I've been tempted to call since the split. But I won't do it. Mainly because I'm not sure I could formulate words and get them out of my mouth.

What I'd like is to be able to talk with him in that light, fun, comforting way again. But that's over. As long as he chooses her over me then I can't know him. Even if he gets rid of her now because he realizes he's lost a treasure, he still can't fix things. It can't ever go back to how it was because the pain can't be undone, ever.

Well, it's not like he's got any desire, or has made any effort, to change the situation, beg my forgiveness and win me back.

My heart hurts.

February 22nd

Please just let this be PMS. I feel like I'm going backward. Is it because everyone knows now, and since it's fresh for them, it has to be fresh for me? Am I moving into a new phase of grief where I have to feel everything acutely? Haven't I already done that? I'm already angry. Do I have to be shattered again as well? Is the reeling ever going to be at an end? How much longer do I have to live in fear of this backing up on me? Months? Years? I thought I was getting on with my life. I was feeling pretty good. At least it seemed like it.

Now I think I miss him. I'm crushed again at the thought of him with the woman he chose over me. I'm thinking about him and wondering about him a lot. I'm going backwards.

The only thing I'm not doing (and hopefully won't do) is wanting him back, wanting my life with him back. When I think of him coming to his senses, it gives me no pleasure. There are no fantasies involving his groveling and me deigning to take him back. I guess I'm lucky in that.

What was between us has been destroyed, pulverized by him. There is no going back. I guess I'm lucky in that, too.

Maybe that's what hurts. That knowledge. Recognizing that there will never be a way to make this okay. It will always be an injustice done against my love, my heart and my soul. What's done is done. Now could the pain that accompanies the injury please start receding? When is the hurt going to run out?

If only all the pain did something useful, like burn calories... I'd look incredible right now!

Here's the worst thing, the part I can't ever admit to anyone – it sickens me to even write it here, but I need it to be somewhere else besides my heart. Here it is:

He didn't want me with him in Las Vegas. He wanted her there. He didn't want me to be part of his birthday celebration. He wanted to share it with her. He told me he didn't want a fortieth birthday party. And then he went to Vegas for a blowout party with all his friends, without me! Did he REALLY think he would get away with it? And get away with having her there as his girlfriend and not me?!!!

Not only did he never really love me (which he basically said to me last November), but the hard, ugly truth is that he never wanted to claim me as the woman in his life. He didn't want his friends to know me or know about me.

In short, for six years, I was just a booty call.

I wasn't good enough for him to want me on his arm. He never wanted to be seen as my date. More than once, he told people (in front of me) that they were mistaken in thinking we were dating.

Good god, why did I put up with that?! You know, I don't even remember fighting about that. I should've taken his head off for it!

I made his life so much better. He readily took my love, my friendship, my concern and my efforts to help, but I was just a dirty little secret, an embarrassing appendage. He could seem to love and care for me, as long as it stayed between us. But he could never accept or claim me in public. I wasn't good enough.

For six years I loved someone with everything I had, and that someone was ashamed of me.

How shattering is that? Pretty darn, I'd say.

February 25th

I laughed with him more than anybody else. He could wear my nerves so thin – he wasn't easy – but then he was. We talked in shorthand. We had so many silly jokes. There's no one else like him in my life, and that's as a friend. I miss the friendship. I miss that person who makes me laugh. But that's gone too.

Collateral damage.

I wish so much to have that part back, but it was destroyed with all the rest. It can't exist anymore. The lying, cheating, rejecting boyfriend wiped it out in his wake of destruction. A scorched earth policy, his march across my heart.

However much he's feeling in the way of sorrow or regret, it's not enough for him to want to fix it, fix us. Which hurts so horribly. It's such a slap in the face. But thank God for it, 'cause I can't ever take him back. There's no more forgiveness left for him, ever.

February 26th

Here's a new one:

I woke up this morning thinking about where I was five years ago. After the whole old-girlfriend-from-college episode – he denies her, yells at me, it takes me two weeks of begging his forgiveness before he'll allow me back. And then what do I do? Chump that I am, I forgive him.

Well, sorta. See, he never really apologized for that. He never was contrite.

But somehow I ended up at his place again. And I found that he had replaced the picture of us from my boss's party with a picture of him with the old-girlfriend-from-college. I did something I've never done in any relationship – I threw the frame across the room, and prepared to storm out. And then he did something which, when I look back on it now, seems extraordinary, and I hate him for doing it.

He stopped me and took me into his arms and talked sweetly to me, and I stayed. For five more years.

Okay, it was stupid of me to even have gone back there, but really, how could I have forgiven that?

The answer is, I haven't. I haven't ever gotten over that. He was a super-class shitheel. Was I really such a dimwit that all it took was a small semblance of contrition from him, holding me tenderly so I wouldn't leave, talking to me so endearingly, to make me believe he truly loved and valued me?

I can say I was young, but I was twenty-six. Young-ish, maybe, but shouldn't I have been a little savvier about men?

I wonder more about why I stayed on than how I stayed on, although I do marvel at the latter.

The thought of being around him now makes me sick. I live in fear of bumping into him in public, because I'm pretty sure looking him in the eye would be impossible; I can't imagine doing anything but bursting into tears and throwing up.

I keep telling myself I never ran into him once during the two months last year when we weren't speaking, after he refused to come visit my parents with me. But I would've been able to handle it then. Now I know I can't, so I'm sure I'm going to manifest it for myself.

Anyway, here's the new bit:

I wish I could go back to five years ago, break free of his arms, walk out that door and never look back. If I had done that, odds are I would've met someone else. Maybe had kids. Had a house with a dog or two. I would've had love and affection and good sex for the last five years. And maybe it also would have ended at some point. But even then, it would have been something real, something meaningful.

He has made it clear, he's never had any attachment or fidelity to me. He never altered the course of his life one iota because of me.

But his life for the last few years would have been far worse without me, or with any other woman, because no woman could have seen him through the tough times with as much love and care as I did. Who knows what misery he would be in now if it wasn't for me? And that isn't an exaggeration.

So I'm trying to tell myself that this is why I was meant to follow this path, that it's more than just a really, really hard life lesson to learn. I did something selfless. Only thing is, it wasn't on purpose. I wasn't a saint. I was stupid.

I've always believed things happen for a reason. I also believe that there's no point in regrets, no room for "if onlys".

But today, for the first time ever, I'm giving myself a real ask-kicking for a choice I made five years ago. Partly because I honestly can't fathom the process of how I got to where I could live with what he'd done. I honestly cannot recall more than a memory of some pain, some tears, but it must have hurt as much as it did this time. It's like I've blocked it all out to preserve my sanity.

How could I have managed to put aside his infidelity and carry on with him?

And for God's sake, why?!

I think being dazzled by him was only a part of it – he was just so damn charming and charismatic! The main thing, though, I think, was my pride. I was not going to be tossed aside and undervalued. Staying meant I was the chosen one. My vanity and pride got me where I am today.

Maybe if I had been closer to my girlfriends, not put up a wall, trusted them more, I would've shared the pain when it happened, and they could have done the girlfriends' duty and gotten me away from him.

But what did any of us know?

It's only been this time around that I truly understood what Beth went through with her first fiancé. Even though they never married, when they broke up, she said it was like going through a divorce. That's where I am now. And I'm not sure there's many who would understand that. Well, my girlfriends probably would've understood enough five years ago to get me away from a jerk I had invested six months in (as opposed to six years).

So I'm wishing that break-up book I'm reading now had been around for that first break up. Maybe it would have knocked some sense into me. I want to jump back in time to that living room and grab that girl's arm, pull her away from the jerk and out the door, saying to her, "This morning you're starting a new life. Forget that guy. Forget him now. You don't have anything to prove to anyone, not even yourself. This shit happens. Go find someone worthy of you. Guaranteed he'll be a better man than this. And, even more, he'll love you a lot more than this one ever will."

Is this why I'm so stuck right now? That this big pile of regret has been trying to surface for me to deal with?

Does everyone go through this? When they're living through a break-up, does every bit of buried crap come up, along with exciting, surprising, thoroughly horrific new ways to look at it?

As I said, there are no "if onlys" in this life. And yet I so much want to rewrite the past.

HOW DID I MANAGE TO STAY?!?! HOW???? WHY?!!!!

I cannot for the life of me figure out how I swallowed that heartache and continued with him. How? How? And what possessed me? In God's name, what was I thinking? Honestly, I'm asking you, Universe, what was I thinking? Truly, I am bewildered.

How refreshing to have these new realizations to wake up to, just when I was starting to get so very bored with the familiar loop of painful thoughts playing endlessly in my brain.

She's only twenty-six. Somebody help her before she ruins her life. Leave the cold, careless man. Please, somebody save her!! Let her have a good life.

... Somebody save her. She's only thirty-one. Let her have a good life.

I guess I have the answer, now that I have stopped and sobbed – a big, gasping, cathartic sobbing.

Everything happens for a reason, including the surfacing of old baggage. I just stopped and cried for myself at twenty-six, and at thirty-one. Nothing or no one could have done much to change things for me. There were plenty of times in the past when people offered their concerned thoughts, but there was no talking me away from him. It was all up to me, something I had to do myself. Just like it is now.

I can't help that twenty-six-year-old girl, but I can perform a long-overdue intervention on this thirty-one-year-old woman.

Darling, you've wasted all the time and tears you're going to on this one. He gets no more of them. Darling girl, it's time for you to look for happiness, and maybe love. Don't fight it, because you're getting dragged away from a painful place. The choice is made for you. You are not going back in there.

Feel the hand on your arm. You're being pulled to safety and a new, better life. You're a young woman with lots of living ahead of you. And you will be very happy. There's so much out there for you.

Stop thinking about him You have better things to do with your time, and your life.

For today is a beautiful, crisp, sunny day. It's a big, lovely world out there this morning. And you're going out there in it. You won't be alone. You've got this older, wiser you looking after you now.

And I promise I will never fail to look after you again.

Sometimes I think I'm really slow to figure things out.

March

March 2nd

You would think that after my epiphany, I would be doing better. But I spent a number of hours over the last few days sobbing into a washcloth. I'm trying to work out if there is a finite (albeit enormous) amount of pain I have to feel before it's all gone. If so, I hope the stockpiles of heartache are almost depleted. How wretched will I be if I've only begun to make a dent in them.

Is there a scientific formula for all this? A quantifiable amount? Heck, I'd settle for an algorithm at this point.

Let's see, what have I been crying over?

Mostly familiar ground.

I've been awfully upset about the other woman, and how he chose her over me. I replayed the airport dumping scene and the weekend he and I slept in the same bed and he wouldn't touch me, and I had to feel the humiliation of knowing, other woman or not, he was afraid that someone might think I was important to him, that he could be attracted to me and want me with him.

That is truly the worst part of this, the part that makes me want to scream at him.

Why does he get to view me as not good enough?

I don't think my hurt is coming because of my love for him. I did love him and wanted him around and to be mine, but I think all this hurt is because I feel betrayed, lied to, and rejected. He did not value me. He had no respect for me. And he should've.

But that is his flaw, not mine. He has a poor character. He's not a very good person. He is a selfish, spoiled, self-destructive person.

He has had a lot of pain in his life. But he has caused a great deal of pain himself, and thought very little about doing so.

I want him to be in pain, and be torn up with guilt for hurting dear, wonderful me so badly and so callously. What are the odds that he's feeling anything at all? What are the odds that it even pops into his mind, let alone pokes at his heart? Nil, wouldn't you suppose?

When we were apart last year, he claimed afterwards to have shed some tears over losing me. Bullshit, most likely, but I do wish it was so. I'd like to think that six years made some imprint on his heart, even if he didn't want it to.

He's been so calm and understanding since the break-up. Like he knows he's been caught and there's no more lying, and he's been allowed to give up the charade.

He's probably relieved.

After all, he didn't have to do the breaking up.

He was effective enough at being a cold asshole that he successfully managed to force me into having to pull the trigger and say the words.

I have to find a way to make this recede into the past, to start counting him as just another ex. I feel exhausted by this pain. I can't control the hurt or anger, or when it surfaces. I really can't control the tears. I feel like I'm worse off than I was at the beginning.

I was coming out of the bookstore today and a man opened the door to come in as I was going. He looked at me like I was pretty. Nice looking guy. I smiled and thanked him for holding the door for me, and secretly was profoundly grateful for the reminder that other men will be attracted to me and appreciate me.

Right now I don't trust any of them, but I'll accept their attentions and compliments, and be immensely thankful for them. It helps me.

March 4th

I'm doing better today. It seems like thinking through some of these things can go either way for me. It ends either in epiphany or breakdown.

I know I feel better when I "rub him out of the roll call." I'm starting to believe that I think about him in order to keep him in the present, to hang onto our relationship, but all I'm doing is keeping the pain and trespasses alive and fresh.

I haven't been thinking about him as much for the last two days (I've also taken to rubbing my reflexology points for the pituitary gland to try to help calm and balance my frazzled brain), and I'm feeling lighter and more joyful. Like I'm stepping clear of the pain field. That's what it is – a pain minefield, where one misstep can cause a terrible, unexpected blast. But hopefully I'm clear of it, or getting close.

Please, God, let me keep going in this direction.

March 5th

Spent the whole day cleaning and working – never rested for more than a few minutes – and it helped, but I'm still having thoughts and moments of longing and sadness. Little things stick at me, reminders of past injuries, his bad attitude at times, all the things he refused to do with me. The only blessing regarding that last part is that I can pretty much go anywhere and do anything and not have memories of us together. So there's one hotel in San Francisco I would be melancholy to see again. Maybe a couple of memories from New York. But mostly my memories are from inside his house.

I don't think I'm missing him, but I'm missing the laughs, the comfort, the routine, the security. I miss feeling close to someone, and he was usually very charming and fun. But now I can only think of him with that new woman, being happier in her company than with me. I pray that won't be the case for long. I don't want him to be sad and alone, but I want his choice of her over me to prove to be a dreadful, wretched mistake.

Him with her. I just feel so angry and sick when I think of it. And I really, really hate being this person. I want to be better than this. But I'm just a wounded, petty mess.

It sure seems like thinking about it enough would start to deaden the pain, but it doesn't. The only thing I can do is block it out as much as possible.

I'm so glad I can say this stuff here. It's all too ugly and pathetic to share with anyone. I couldn't bear for anyone to know I'm taking this so badly.

I've seen my girlfriends go through break-ups, but they manage to handle them like grown-ups – sad, yes, but not petty.

Or maybe they have secret journals of their own, where they say things just like this?

In that break-up book I'm reading, there's a part where a woman describes her girlfriends pulling away and not supporting her after she went to her ex's house and burned her name into his lawn with fertilizer.

So maybe, on balance, I'm doing okay.

At least I'm not her. And I won't be. I won't dream of giving my ex that satisfaction.

March 8th

All those months he lied to me and dated someone else while pulling away and becoming critical of me. He was distant and increasingly indifferent, until he would have a pang of guilt. Sometimes there was caring, but mostly it came after a big push-away. He would insist he cared in order to keep me on the ropes. I guess I was the back-up plan, old faithful, in case things didn't work out in his real relationship.

I guess he cared some since he acted like he still wanted me around when I was prepared to go. Although that could have been as much about his need to get rid of me distress- and guilt-free as it was about any genuine regard he had for me.

I wish so much for that note of validation – a few written words professing his love, respect, gratitude. How great a person I am. How sorry he is. How much hurt (and perhaps guilt) he feels. I wish I could know that at least he has given this some thought, and that he felt this way, even if only a little bit.

TI did so much. I loved so much. I don't deserve this pain.

March 11th

I think he's traveling today to that conference. She probably took him to the airport. She has stepped into my place, my life. Oh, shit, I sound like Betty Broderick.

Or maybe he let her go with him – the conference is in New Orleans, after all. He would never have taken me, but maybe he takes her with him on his trips.

Despite the hurt, I still want to know him. But only when the pain is gone, which, right now, feels like forever. I still get sickened if I think on it too much.

I'd like to get through a day without wanting to cry (although I am gaining some small amount of control over my flow of tears). I'd like to sleep through the night without some painful thought jolting me awake so I can lie there unable to go back to sleep, feeling sad (or in despair when it's really bad).

The only mercy is that I'm able to shut it all down when I go into work. I'm glad my job doesn't require a lot of interaction with others most of the time. I can manage a friendly "hello" and an occasional question.

But what a relief it is to get home at the end of the day and take the mask off!

March 21st

I'm doing okay. Last weekend was the beginning of the lessening of grief. By Monday I was feeling indifference, and hardly thinking of him at all. It stayed that way most of this week, with only a twinge now and then.

He's drifting out of my thoughts.

That does seem to make a big difference. I don't know why it happened, but it's like someone turned off the free-flowing tap of pain and horrendous thoughts. At least I hope that is the right analogy. I hope that it's not a pain river that's been dammed up and will eventually burst. Because that last bout of misery was in some ways worse than the first.

Initial heartache is painful, but it is doing a job – it takes one to a new place. Everyone understands.

But having backslides is just grizzly, and it's really asking a lot of people to be sympathetic.

Repeat heartache feels like it's just doing damage.

Please, God, let this be the beginning of my new, happy life.

No more unbearable pain.

No more tears.

He's just one man, after all.

He isn't everything.

March 23rd

Writing seems to help, and I feel the need to do it tonight, although I'm not sure what to say. The only new thought I had today was, in being out in the world, not one single man was attractive to me. I feel like I'm lacking something, missing something, but I'm absolutely cold to the notion of being close to any man. I don't want the last one, but I don't want the new one, either.

How is it that guys don't seem to have this problem after a break-up? I've known a number of guys who have had their hearts completely crushed, and then they're back dating again within a few weeks. And not just a hook-up, or transition person, but a new relationship. I can't imagine being able to do that.

I feel unsettled tonight. I have had thoughts about him, but it's because I feel like he misses me. I sense his missing me, perhaps with a little sadness. I'm hoping for it.

Yes, it sounds loony, and I'm probably clutching at straws, but I figure whatever it takes to get me through this.

Part of me wishes so much for contact, but when it happens it only upsets me, and for a good while. I have a much better chance of getting through this with grace and dignity if I say nothing.

The good news is that the tiniest bit of progress has been made in turning him back from the sun, moon, heavens and stars, into just a regular guy again.

Because, after all, he is just a guy.

One of the billions who have lived and died, worked and loved and breathed, since the dawn of mankind.

The universe no longer orbits around him.

He is not the gatekeeper and keyholder to all that is wondrous and magical and exciting about life.

The world does not belong to him nor operate for his pleasure.

It is entirely possible for marvelous, delightful, joyous things to happen without his hand in them.

I'd like to think it speaks well of me that I can foster such grand delusions about a person when I love them... but I'm not sure it does.

March 27th

Weepy girl is back. I'm wishing for the comfort of him (how many times have I said that?! How many times have I been right here?!). He knows me so well (doesn't always approve of who I am, but...). I didn't wear a mask with him. I feel like I do with everyone else, except my family. I didn't have to pretend with him. Of course, it took a lot of energy to be with him in other ways, but I didn't have to put on my social mask. I could just be me. And that is a biggie.

I went from feeling good, feeling like he misses me to "Don't you miss me at all?" I want to tell him that I miss him, and earlier I was willing to. Then I got that image of him with someone else. And, even more, that flashback of him hugging me with indifference, as he made up some excuse for why he was pulling away. The pain of that stopped me cold. Maybe he did still care about me. Maybe he still does. But I believe now that he had grown indifferent, and was keeping me around for insurance, and that was only if he could control how much or little of me he had to contend with. Too much of me and I'd be gone, insurance be damned.

The other, and probably more accurate, theory is that he was fine with me until he met someone who really stirred him. He said his feelings for me hadn't changed – which means they never were very much – but he didn't mind the tepidness until something truly passionate showed up. Then he realized what we lacked, or simply moved on from our subsistence-level relationship.

I guess I had believed in my heart that he simply didn't recognize love, that what we had was "too peaceful to be love" like I'd read about before in some obviously clueless self-help book. How young and naïve can a person be? I really thought I had more smarts than that.

Somehow I convinced myself that he'd been blind to his feelings. But the truth is, he knew his heart, and I just didn't do it for him. He liked me enough to keep me around, despite his better judgment. But he didn't love me. He said he couldn't love anyone, but obviously he has feelings for her. Feelings strong enough to make him choose her over me.

I don't believe for a moment that he let me go purely for my own well-being, as he claims. He had already pushed me away before I walked.

Why couldn't he have done the decent thing and sent me packing as soon as he knew he wasn't interested in me (as in five years ago)? Why couldn't he have been a good enough person to put my feelings before his own selfish needs?

There's a chance that he feels bad about those "selfish years" he kept me around when he knew it was wrong.

But I have to take ownership of my part in this: he told me from the beginning he couldn't have a relationship with anyone, and hearing that, I chose to stay. He didn't have a hope of getting rid of me.

The thing is, it turns out he could have a relationship with someone. Just not with me. He didn't want me. He didn't ever love me. God, what a horrible thing to have to accept!

It's stuff like that which would tear me to bits if I had to say it out loud.

I'm sure he doesn't like that I'm heartbroken. I'm hoping that his silence is to protect me and help me, and not out of convenience for him or indifference to me. But who am I kidding? I remember reading somewhere that's it's really so very easy for the jilting party to move on, while the one who has been rejected is still flailing around.

I guess this makes for a whole new aspect of heartbreak. I hadn't been sad about the possibility that he really didn't love me. I might've thought it, but I didn't believe it. Now I do.

What's really awful is, none of this should matter. He's an ex-boyfriend, relegated to the past. Why must I keep circling around with these same useless thoughts? I really, really hate sounding like a broken record. A crazy, obsessive broken record.

What is the secret to making it stop? Anyone? The break-up books offer advice, but I want the quick, surefire remedy. A magic pill.

March 29th

Today I'm exhausted. I slept for only five hours and woke up with a headache. I'm back to having Kleenex with me all the time. And I can't get the words down right. I really just want to stay in bed all day, but I'm not going to do it. That weak little voice inside that is me looking out for me, is getting louder, and it's strong enough now to propel me forward even when I'm exhausted physically, mentally and emotionally.

In a weird way I envy addicts that go to rehab facilities (I'm talking about the nice ones, like Betty Ford or the swanky Promises in Malibu). When someone reaches their bottom, they go away from the world, to a place of seclusion and protection, where everyone there understand they're in trouble and in pain. I'm sure it's tough and challenging, but there are parts to it that sound good. The person no longer has any outside world responsibilities, like bills to pay or a job to show up to. They get to deal with their problems and be upset and wear warm-up suits and have their meals prepared for them. They have people looking after them and people to counsel them. To be understood and looked after, with no distractions from the outside world... everyone should be allowed to have that after a break-up.

I put on make-up like it's a mask and I go out into the world and act as normal as possible, but I get tired and my control begins to slip. And I start to wonder if people can see me. If I talk to a sales clerk, can they see my pain? Do my eyes betray me? My expression? The way I move? Do they see my hidden truth? I feel it all starting to slip, and I feel exposed. Are they gentler because I seem weak, or can they see the trouble?

Most people are so caught up in their own lives that they don't see anyone else's troubles. I include myself here. I can't recall being struck by someone else's sadness, but no doubt it's there. I think we all are likely not to notice a stranger's pain. I actually hope no one notices me. Sometimes the effort is too great and I can't hide my feelings. Thank goodness people are not aware enough to see it. It's like hiding in plain sight.

March 31st

For the past few days I've been haunted by the sense of him with her. My peace of mind longs for them to be done, for him to have discovered her faults and sent her packing. I pray for it to happen. But I still wouldn't have him back. I just want him to feel like he was a fool to choose her over me.

What makes me feel physically sick is knowing he was with her – the new, shiny, wonderful woman, and working to push me away. How pathetic I must've seemed to him – the idiot who didn't know what was happening, continuing along, accepting scraps, accepting his flimsy stories, offering love and affection that wasn't welcome.

All those times I kissed him and touched him and had sex with him, and he was wishing it wasn't me. Fantasizing that it was her. God, how revolting! The thought of him having to endure my touch, endure my presence... it makes me so sick, so close to dry-heaving.

I still feel so broken-hearted. It must be better, though, 'cause the pain isn't front and center and constant. But I'm still crying. Two months since I told him, "no more," and here I am in tears. No one knows that I'm still in this much pain.

I think most everyone feels I should either be over it or – since I've been so private about it – that I'm over it already. No one ever thought he was a great guy. They certainly thought I should find someone else. So it's hard for them to muster sympathy for my pain, or at least muster very much.

But they have all been exceedingly kind. They truly love me, and I love them.

Today I saw that Leslie has put a few posts on Facebook over the last two days, announcing to the world that she and Bill are done. I can't imagine being that open about it! She's shared some of her pain and a few snarky remarks, but somehow she's managed to say all the gracious stuff I wish I could muster – amicable separation, wishing him well, etc.

Is it better to broadcast one's heartache, which demands the sympathy, or at least feigned sympathy, of friends? Does a person heal faster? Feel better? Or down the road, do they regret airing their private details? I must say, Leslie knows how to wear heartbreak well.

At least to the outside world, she appears to have a grip on her "disappointment" and seems to be moving on. The most she's done is look a little pale. I'm sure I'm not giving out that vibe. I really wish I could handle this with more grace, or at least be a grown-up. Instead I burst into tears in public, and at home I spend entire weekends in the same smelly sweats.

Sometimes I feel like I'm dying inside, and no one can see it, or wants to see it. I feel so, so alone. I want so much to stay in bed, but my pride pushes me forward. At least my ridiculous pride is making itself useful.

I know part of the "her-over-me" pain is the humiliation of feeling lied to and rejected, and feeling like he was forced to endure me.

But a big part of the pain comes from my pride being hurt. I look at photos of him, and even at his most handsome and charming, I feel no desire to have him back. I miss only the laughter and comfort, and not the handsome man. My small life feels even smaller.

April

April 2nd

I'm worn down, drained of my energy. The tears took all my spirit with them. I feel empty, but it's a calm empty. I don't feel happy, but I'm not sad either. I feel nothing, but I'm not numb. Really, just empty.

I feel lost. And scared. And pretty much alone. Thank God for my parents. They got me through today, with all my confusion and angst.

I feel so weak and so helpless in controlling my tears. I'm backsliding again. Again.

April 8th

What a difference a week makes. I'm not about to get cocky, but I'm feeling *so* much better. And I'm not thinking about or feeling much for him. He's leaving my brain and heart, and his lack of feeling for me doesn't seem to hurt so much.

It's scary to let go of the thoughts and pain, because it means the relationship really is over and becoming part of the past – no more present, definitely no future. That's a tough one to swallow. But when you can finally start letting go, oh, it feels so much better!

It is almost uncomfortable for me to crack open this Book of Crazy, and see where I've been. But it hasn't thrown me. Neither has putting together the box of his things which I'm mailing tomorrow. Without a note. He will know what it is.

Again, I'm not getting cocky. No chance of that. I've thought I was out of the woods before, only to rubber band stretch and snap back into the pain.

What has changed everything is a job opening in Hawaii. I went from being scared to being exhilarated. A week ago I felt like my prospects were bleak. Now I'm excited. The only thing I will have to worry about is how will I get everything packed and purged so I can head out on time? I believe that job is mine. A new life in paradise. A fresh start. All the bad memories carried away on tropical breezes. And of course I'm hoping to find love on the island.

I feel like my life is leading me to that magical world. Everything is aligning itself so I can go off to my new life. All the hurt, disappointment and betrayal of the last year has been there to force me to break away and leave for my exciting new life. No more quiet, small world for me!

April 12th

I made it through a minefield yesterday. That's when he would have received the box of his stuff. But he didn't email or call, so I think I won't hear from him at this point. He was getting into my thoughts a bit, but I really panicked that he might contact me. However he feels about me, or any new woman in his life, doesn't matter. I am free and I can go live in paradise and be happy. I know Kauai is making a place for me. I know it. I feel it.

I went out for Thai food with the girlfriends, and focused all my attentions on talking about their lives and what's been happening with them. They all have their own things going on – some good, some bad. I was glad to hear all of it. Such a good reminder that I'm not the center of the world, that life keeps going, and that everyone has a saga.

They did ask me about my situation, and I told them a bit of the story (up until now, I've avoided giving any details, because doing so makes me start crying and also because it's unbearably humiliating to reveal what an enormous idiot I've been). I didn't go into it much, but it was enough for my wonderful, loyal girlfriends to denounce him as a despicable jerk and call me a saint for putting up with him. All the usual sentiments, all the right things to say – "You're too good for him," "He didn't deserve you," "You're so much better off now," "Thank God you got away from him," etc. All good stuff, all so reassuring. Your girlfriends are what get you through the bad times.

I think it was in one of the Bridget Jones' books where she said that if Miss Havisham in *Great Expectations* had possessed a group of girlfriends, after she was jilted on her wedding day, they would've taken her out for cocktails, and she wouldn't have spent the rest of her life holed up in her dining room, wearing a tattered wedding dress.

So God bless the girlfriends!

Still, what I realized after I left dinner was that I have no wish to share their feelings about him as a person – the despicable jerk part, he's an asshole, he's a piece of shit (even though I'm pretty sure I've said that about him – or maybe I only said he had acted like an asshole... anyway...).

I don't need to make him a villain to get on with my life. And I don't want to carry that anger in me. The wound will never heal if I do. As they say, forgiveness is not for the other person, it's for you.

(It's also possible that the vain, proud part of me doesn't want to declare him a jerk, because then it makes me the loser who stayed with a jerk for six years.)

Aside from all that, as I said, I am finally ridding myself of the angst and obsessive thoughts, of the unpredictable, uncontrollable tears, of the anguish and heartbreak. I feel lighter, happier.

I have such excitement and hope in my heart that I find myself hesitating to open this journal, even to put down healthy, positive words, because I don't want to touch or feel that pain I went through. Maybe my new words can neutralize all that ugliness. Maybe the energy, the chi of this journal can be altered.

It's been hard-fought and hard-earned, but I'm truly better. I've rounded the corner. He is an ex, and I'm growing more indifferent daily. My life and happiness await me somewhere else, and I am so very glad of it!

April 16th

I'm glad I put down those more positive words, because they cheered me when I read them just now.

Maybe it's the novelty wearing off my plan that is causing diminished euphoria. Maybe it's eating ice cream. PMS. But I'm a bit down and feeling a bit haunted by old pains.

I've been cleaning out my storage space and, in doing so, I discovered a long-forgotten journal I'd started about our love affair. It was only about twenty pages, and it seems to have been written in the first couple of months of our dating. Funny thing is, I have absolutely no memory of having that journal or writing anything down.

I didn't read the whole thing, but there was stuff I couldn't recall happening, like him being really sweet and making me feel special. He must've been into having fun and romance until he became bored or the relationship was no longer new, and then he became cold, aloof guy with all the damage. Or else I projected loveliness onto him that he really didn't possess.

And did he really make love to me four times that first night? 'Cause, wow, I *really* don't remember that!

The thing is, there's a lapse in the journal. I stopped writing, and then picked it up again months later, after he had altered. And there I said that I thought the best part, the fun, romantic part was over, and I didn't believe it would ever be that good again.

So why did I stay? As in, why in the hell did I stay? As in WTF?

I did get other things from our relationship, but I'm beginning to feel it was more of a learning experience than a relationship. An ass-kicker of a learning experience. That big fat lesson I needed to be taught.

That poor, foolish girl writing those words in that journal.

To be so blinded by that dazzling man.

Now here she sits, six years later, thirty-something, overweight, exhausted and starting to look old, with a patched-together heart. And I'm back to wondering just how much or how little I actually penetrated his heart. It shouldn't matter, but it does.

He doesn't want me anymore, or need me. I feel like a repulsive, wretched creature. Pathetic.

I hate to think he sees me this way, but it's even worse that I do, that I've let his treatment of me make me view myself like this.

I was too adoring and giving for him to ever respect me. I tried to be the perfect girlfriend, and it turned me into a doormat. Why couldn't I have understood a lot sooner that he didn't want a doormat, that no man wants a doormat?

The thing that sets him apart is his selfishness. Most men, after becoming bored, would do the decent thing and either drop me or ghost me. But he is too spoiled and greedy, and careless with others' feelings. What's so aggravating about his rotten behavior is that he really seemed to believe he never put a foot wrong. Whatever the fight, it was always my fault that he wound up acting like an asshole.

At least the break-up book is right in saying, those annoying things he did will never bother me again. That is a comfort, and a most-welcome silver lining to all this.

(I want to stop the flow of negative thoughts and energy before it gets too strong. It's not good for me and I don't need it.)

I shredded those journal pages. Someday I'll probably shred these, too. I'm not sure I believe in keeping a written record of this devastating heartbreak for posterity.

Usually when I go back and re-read my thoughts, I just feel uncomfortable. The only pleasure I get is in picturing where and who I was when I was recording my thoughts in the first place, and hopefully seeing that I've made significant progress.

This journal, this Book of Crazy, has really helped to pull me through my pain, and I'm so glad there's still some room left, because obviously I am still haunted. But that's really all it feels like – the ghost of the excruciating pain of his rejection and his dumping me for another woman.

My life now is (or should be) with a Jolly Book of Happiness and Dreams, not with the Book of Crazy. That is where I wish to spend my time. But it would seem I still need to make an occasional appearance here. What little pain I have left goes here. I don't want to share it or talk about it, because it all comes out as random, high school-sounding gibberish.

And also, it's almost like, if I talk about my past relationship, it somehow dilutes it. Somehow it doesn't belong to me as much.

Or maybe I just got too used to this happy new feeling of living without pain, and I don't want to do anything to weaken this delicate ground I am currently treading upon.

April 18th

A bad truth about me and this relationship: I hung on way, way too long, until finally it took something as extreme as him going off with another woman to finish us. Because I was never going to sever the ties on my own.

Truth be told, it's how I've always been. I don't stay in situations because they're satisfying. I stay because I've invested so much, and I'm waiting for the big payoff... or at least some sort of reasonable return on my investment.

But guess what? Apparently relationships don't work the same way back accounts or blue-chip stocks do. How foolish am I?!

Time to cut my losses and count my blessings.

April 21st

A little melancholy.

I've been dealing with the idea of that other woman, and what if she isn't so great but he still picked her over me?

I tried to tell myself that he worked very hard to keep me in his life, even if it meant lying to me, but let's be honest – when it came down to her or me, he didn't hesitate to let me go.

So, in essence, I wasn't worth him giving her up, even though it meant losing me.

I guess he could say I didn't give him the option. I just left and told him to leave me alone. And I meant it. But he didn't try even a little bit to get me back. After our six years together, he just let me go.

I'm sure he will forever stick with saying it was the best thing for me, and hopefully that will prove to be true.

But he can't fool me.

He didn't let me go for my benefit.

He never did anything for my benefit.

This was all about him having things the way he wanted.

It's been three months since the break-up and I'm still wondering if I ever was anything special to him.

I'm getting teary, and I want to know why. Why am I still going over this ground? Why do I still hurt? I don't want him back.

I don't really think I want to know him anymore. He's difficult.

And I end up feeling crummy and worried and depressed.

Why won't my pride let go? Yes, he was a fool. He made bad choices. And he's lost me forever, which is terrible for him.

Fate forced this.

No, I forced Fate to take me here. This has to be painful or I won't let go and start my fabulous new life. This has to be egregious and irrevocable, to make me do what I've needed to do for the last two years.

April 30th

This is as close as I've been to backsliding, wanting to talk with him. No question, if I had been liquored up last night, I would've drunk-dialed him.

It was the stresses at work which were doing it — some days are just really crappy, and I miss my confidante, but I can't talk to him about my work problems anymore. He would just be aloof, and I would hear her influence in what he says, and it will all be hurtful and wrong.

I have to weather this all on my own.

God please let me get that Hawaii job!!

Summer

May 5th

I'm hoping my decision to go off the pill for a while was a good one. It's been a week of withdrawal and I'm hoping my upset was due to a shock to my hormone balance. I've felt good for the last few days, and not really given him much thought (those two things seem to be closely connected).

But not thinking about him is like losing him, and I guess, in some way, I want to feel like he's still there, in the present, that we are still bonded. And of course, I want him to think about me.

There is next-to-no pain in these thoughts, but it's Thursday night and I'm wondering if he's thought about me at all, and that I should be there like I was for all those other Thursday nights. Does he miss me at all? Is he ever sad about me? Does he have any idea how much I hurt, and that I miss him, and how I wish things were different? Does he assume I'm still grieving, or that I'm over it? Does he even ever give me a thought?

I'm okay.

Time to go for a walk and be part of the world.

May 17th

Been doing pretty well, but I've had a few moments here and there where I'm somewhat melancholy, and it can really start to stick me if I think about things too much.

Like, will we ever be able to know each other again? Be in the same room? Be cordial? I can't imagine how things can ever be okay again, let alone us being as close as we were. We will never be friendly exes.

One thing is for sure: the relationship as we knew it is destroyed forever. It will never be what it was, even if we ever do know each other again.

Forget what he thinks is best for me (read "best for him"). Isn't there any part of him that regrets pushing me away?

Regrets his choice?

Doesn't he ever wish he could have me back?

Or did I really come to mean so little to him that he doesn't feel my absence at all?

I think it's me having to accept the nasty truth that for years he kept me around for the sake of convenience, when he wasn't truly interested in me.

He only decided to do the "right thing" and not string me along anymore when he met her, and I became superfluous. He wasn't ending our relationship because he didn't want to string me along; he wanted to be done with me because I was in the way.

And he didn't even end it, I did! He didn't have the balls to break up with me, and instead just made things so miserable between us that I was forced into having to do the deed myself. What a chickenshit way to handle things, dude!!!

I made it so easy on him. I did all of the heavy lifting. All he had to do was walk away. No, not even that. He only had to stay in place was like the center of the universe that he is, while I made the long, slow painful march away from him.

Starting to go to the dark place. Which is worse – to push the thoughts out of my head, or let them run their course? Is my brain purging itself or obsessing?

Why do I still care so much? Why must I have these thoughts? He is part of my past – albeit a big, dramatic chapter, one which I'm starting to feel ashamed and embarrassed about.

June 1st

So much of the pain is gone, but I still get twinges, which can become real pain if I continue with my thoughts. How do I look at things and sort them out, without sliding into wallowing in them?

I've become haunted by the notion that he came to feel indifferent toward me, that he didn't carry any form of love toward me, that he was no longer even physically attracted to me. Which meant all those nights in bed together, me curled against him, he was hating it. Is that an accurate assessment? I just don't know.

But why should it matter? It's over! No more of this pain! No more sadness!

It's hard on Thursdays – those were our nights, not that we had such an exciting time. But it was our thing, our routine, maybe the only real couple-like thing we did. Now all those recipes we tried out together, he probably cooks for her. It's a stinging revelation, but I'm so thankful this hadn't occurred to me earlier, when I was in the depths of pain. It would have tortured me.

Funny thing is, he doesn't seem so important anymore – not as in "I feel so in control and over him that I'm okay to see him or hear about him". No, it's simply that he just doesn't matter so much these days, except for when I wish I had his shoulder to lean on. But even then, I don't want things back the way they were.

And I truly know, I don't want him back. I still hurt some, but somewhere along the line, without noticing, I actually did move on.

Now if I could just keep him from showing up in my dreams, but I guess my mind has stuff it needs to sort out. Still, I don't like it, no matter whether it's a good dream or a bad one. Both ways leave me feeling upset and rattled. I don't like the idea of him barging into my space uninvited, which is what it feels like.

But clearly it's what my subconscious needs to do right now, and I have to trust that it's only for my own good.

I hate to think of him having a glowing new life with his new girlfriend while I sit here in limbo, praying for that new job and new life – and feeling fat, to boot! It's the latest and hopefully the last piece of angst I have to deal with.

Fuck it all! This has been going on for six months!

He doesn't loom so large anymore, but it still hurts, probably more than it should. Will I ever be over this?!

June 2nd

Why does it I sound like I'm constantly contradicting myself? One sentence I'm fine, the next I'm not?

I guess I just answered my own question.

My sentences come out that way, because that is how quickly my mood changes.

My recovery is such a fragile thing, paper-thin, and it doesn't take more than the slightest disturbance in the air current to rip it to shreds.

Here's what it comes down to: when he lied to me about her, he deliberately chose to make a fool of me.

I can get over my unrequited love. My feelings for him have faded away to only a faint impression of what they used to be. I can even recall good times without sadness.

But what troubles me, what means we will never be okay again, is that he made a fool of me.

And even if he apologizes (an unfathomable notion), he can't ever make it right. He can't erase the choice he made, or the pain it put me through.

This isn't about my ability to forive, or lack thereof.

This is about the fact that who he is as a person means he is incapable of making things right. He doesn't have inside of him what it takes to make an apology or make amends.

And I'm certain he doesn't harbor even the slightest inclination to do so, anyway.

I've had to let him go.

I've had to let go of others in the past.

But this one was brutal, and now I'm coming to understand why: Because I will never know him again, in even the smallest measure.

I don't want to ever know him or see him or speak with him again. This one is truly a goodbye forever.

Silence is my friend, my protector. And let me say it again, just so we're clear (I'm talking to you, my brain, and also to you, my heart):

No matter what, I want nothing to do with him ever again.

June 8th

Maybe it was a bloodletting, all of that last week. All I know is, I've been feeling much lighter, with little obsessing and little pain. I've been smiling at people when I'm out in the world, and I've been laughing when I hear something funny on TV or catch something humorous on the internet.

Which is where I needed to be, since I found out I didn't get the Hawaii job. I'm bereft about it, on a number of levels. First, it was a beautiful, exciting, fresh new start – the perfect palate cleanser. It meant I could start over, with no one knowing my pathetic history. It was a chance to find a good man and begin again. Or be on my own, without having to explain about the ex, without getting any looks of pity (or worse, "I always knew that was headed for a bad end").

It meant I would be safe from him (and her). I wouldn't have to run the risk of bumping into them somewhere in town. I'm certainly not going to monitor his movements on Facebook – I unfollowed him early, and then finally unfriended him, so I couldn't now anyway, even if I could bear doing it.

And going to Hawaii was my chance to say, "My life just got better, now that you're out of it." That was the biggie, and now that's been taken away from me. I really needed it, too. I needed to level the playing field.

He gets to move on, and I'm still stuck. He's happy, I have a broken heart. It's just so lopsided, so horribly unfair. And there's no consolation prize.

June 12th

Fresh new hell and heartache, just when I thought I was done crying.

Rachel emailed me (a very carefully, gently-worded note, an awful email to receive, but thank God she had the guts and the decency to do it – but then a true friend does the hard thing). It seems my ex posted a bunch of pictures on FB of his new home upstate. So I guess that's where she's from, and now they're living together.

After crying to my parents, I drove over to his house. For sale sign. Empty. He's definitely gone.

I don't remember getting back in the car and driving home.

At least I am safe to move freely around town – no more fear of randomly running into him. That will be so nice. I look forward to taking advantage of that as soon as I can stop crying. That should be soon. I've already done heaps of sobbing. There can't be much left.

I don't want to write about this anymore.

June 14th

I'm reeling! New photos on FB apparently – they're engaged!! What the fuck!?!?!?! Shouldn't this complete my pain complete now? How much more of this do I have to take? Hey, maybe she's pregnant! I'm not even sure if it would hurt more or less if she was.

The parents let me cry to them again, but then they told me to just forget him and forget it and move on.

Yeah, no shit?!

What do they think I've been trying to do for the last six months?!

They are right. But then again, they've never been through a heartbreak like this.

They've never been losers.

I remember Jamie once talking about this and saying, "We've all had our heartaches and break-ups and disappointments, but most of us also have that one absolutely crushing relationship, that heartbreak that leaves us shattered and feeling like we'll never get over it."

I've had my share of heartbreaks in the past, but nothing like this.

This one overwhelmed me, overpowered me.

At least I know I will never have this sort of pain again.

I will never let my heart be unprotected again.

I will never again fall in love someone because of their dazzling qualities.

I will only fall in love with them for how they treat me.

There's a line in the movie *Under the Tuscan Sun* where Diane Lane says the worst thing about a divorce (read "crushing break-up) is that it doesn't kill you. It should, but it doesn't.

I know my parents are trying to help, but what I need is loving arms around me, that let me cry, that understand just how wretched, how despairing, how life-altering a break-up can be. But the one person who used to do that for me is now with another woman – his fiancée!

I feel sick. I can't eat. I can't sleep. My mind is racing. I'm worn out. Please God, help me through this.

June 15th

Watching *Angels in America* and heard this quote, or something close to it:

"What does it take for a person to change? Answer: He has to be torn apart and ripped to pieces, and then slowly reassemble himself."

Very fitting.

I'm certain that I'm treading along through another pain minefield, and can have a head-spinning, sharp, stabbing explosion at any moment, and that it will take me a good while to traverse the field and make it to safety.

I'm slowly rebuilding my façade, my countenance. I can go out in public again without fear of uncontrollable tears coming on. Oh, yes, the hurt pride, the broken heart, the shock to the system are all still there, but it's all lessening in healthy amounts. Strangely, it helps to look at old photos of him, because it makes me see a selfish, difficult person who I'd rather not have to deal with.

It's superfluous and silly to be declaring this now, but still, it gives me a sense of power to say, "She can have him. Take him, honey, he's all yours. And no givebacks." It's a comfort to know I mean every word.

June 17th

It's like my heart had scabbed over and was healing, and then the scab got picked off. The wound is oozing, but drying up and starting to scab again. So I guess the trick is not to pick at it.

I won't be telling the parents any more about this. It does no one any good, and they have run out of patience for it. Pop keeps reiterating that this wasn't a real relationship, which I think he believes is helpful, but implies my feelings are less than. And it's not like I can take those hurtful remarks and seek comfort with my ex. That is over, forever. I just wish my heart would understand that fact.

I can't bear the trouble and stress that is him.

Okay, heart, time to let him go.

June 26th

I can't believe I'm actually doing this, but here I am.

I'm visiting my parents so I can help my brother and his wife have a huge yard sale (which includes a lot of my parents' stuff that I've been hauling over from their house). After that's done, whatever doesn't sell gets taken to a couple of charities, and then I'll be helping my brother and sister-in-law move. It's a lot of physical work, but that is a good thing. It's nice to feel physically exhausted instead of emotionally exhausted at the end of the day.

Naturally everyone is focused on getting all the work done, which is right, but there hasn't been one word of comfort or concern towards me about the break-up or my latest heartache. Nothing. It's like they either forgot, or it's too insignificant or too "in the past" to mention. I was supposed to be coming back to an environment where I'd be loved and supported. Ha! This is anything but a safe haven. So I'm here feeling sad and alone.

But I'm beginning to see and understand. Guess who is going to pull me through this... me.

I have me.

That means I get a loving and understanding, fiercely loyal friend who is going to have my back, bolster my spirits and keep me out of harm's way.

This is my grief and my recovery, and I'm gonna own it. I'll do what I have to do. No apologies.

July 3rd

I picture him packing and moving, and driving away with her. Is he still engaged? Have they set a date? Do I ever even enter his mind, even fleetingly?

What's hurting is that part of me is trying to argue that this isn't the end, that I'll know him again. But there really may be nothing else. I have to accept that I may never see or speak with him again.

I said that's what I want, and I meant/mean every word. But now that the reality of that has set in, it's meeting with some resistance. I know the strong me will win out in the end, but I can't help but be a little sorry about it.

How could he have let me go so easily, after six years together? He has never valued me enough to try for me. What a fool I was to love someone so much who didn't love me back.

I must start being happy soon. I want and deserve my turn at a full, happy life.

July 10th

Looking for some comfort after my trip to my parents. Went and saw a psychic today. Had what seems like a very accurate reading. She knew of the heartbreak. It was the first thing she mentioned (of course, there's every possibility that it's written all over my face, in my body language, in my energy, that I'm an open book, a walking disaster area much more than I realize).

She said the heartbreak was the Universe's way of clearing out what wasn't working, and making room for a new man who will love me so much more, and be someone I can trust.

I asked about my ex, and if he felt anything at all. She said he was suffering, that he made a selfish decision and now he was regretting it.

I don't care if she is a fraud, and this is just bullshit – I'm going to hang onto those words for dear life.

She also said she sees me knowing him down the road as a friend, which is a comfort.

The bad part: She said there are still secrets surrounding his decision which I don't know, and that he probably had/has his eye on someone else (did she mean the woman he was with, or another woman besides her? Sheesh!). I said something about him possibly getting married and she didn't say anything. I couldn't read if she just didn't know or if that was an affirmation and she didn't want to tell me because she knew the hysterics which would follow.

But what could she mean by secrets? She said I didn't need to know them in order to move on, and they would just hurt me more. How is that for a mindfuck?

The good news is that he is suffering and knowing he made a bad and wrong decision. Let him suffer.

She said I was stuck and depressed and might not trust that right guy when he shows up, but I'll be very happy with him. She told me to turn my ex's actions over to the Universe and let It square things with him. I am to stay on the path of love and light, and I have many blessings coming to me. What I am not to do is worry.

Thank you, God, for putting her in my path. Her words, however true, were just what I needed. I can heal myself. I'm on my way to better things.

August 18th

I had every intention of letting my last entry be the final entry in this journal, but I needed a safe place to go today. I know my great new life is coming, but I'm hurting and I don't know why. I'm doing as I'm told and letting the Universe deal with him. I am clinging to all the positive visions the psychic had. But still I feel sad and depressed.

Why am I missing someone who caused me pain and left me to deal with it?

Why am I still reliving the pain? My energy and thoughts should be with my new life. The poor Universe is having to drag me like a sit-in protester into my future.

Why can't I stay in the space of looking forward with happy anticipation?

Why does he still have access to my heart? He's gone. He's with someone else. He dumped me. He didn't want me.

How much more do I need to know, do I need to have hit me in the face, before I move on?!!

I'm all stirred up and out of sorts. He shouldn't still be in my thoughts at this point, but I'm not sure how to file him away. How am I supposed to feel about him? How am I supposed to remember him?

All these friggin' questions!

The most enlightened thing I can do is forgive him. I want to be at peace.

My thoughts are all over the place.

I think it got serious enough this afternoon that my grandmother had to come check on me. My apartment smelled like her house when I walked in from the store. That's never happened before. I talked and cried for a little while, and I felt her comfort me. I thanked her for coming, told her I was so glad she came to see me, then told her that she should check on her her daughter, because my aunt needs her more than me right now, and that I'd be okay. I think she is looking out for me, watching over me. One of the last things she ever said to me was simply, "Be happy."

I'm trying to be happy, but must it be such a struggle? Must I have to claw my way there?

I read somewhere that to come back from a break-up is to make a hero's journey. It rings of truth.

I'll figure out how to think about him later, when he is in the past and my heart is safe.

And someday there will be an entry in this journal that is truly the last, when it's all finally and completely over.

The Rest of the Year

October 27th

Just passed the first of the big dates in our calendar, what would've been our seventh anniversary. I spent it at the beach, thinking about how I had wanted to live in a small coastal town, and now he has the life I wished for, but he's having it with someone else. Kinda makes me sick to my stomach.

So much of the pain is gone and whatever does surface, I hand off immediately to the Universe to deal with. What that leaves me with is depression and low self-esteem. I am paralyzed with self-loathing at times. It's difficult to sustain hope and faith. My spirit feels shrunken and empty. I feel unlovable.

It's been nine months. Nine months. Isn't that enough? Haven't I put in enough time by now?

Looking back through these pages, I see that I've come far, and blessedly it reminds me that he can't be in my life ever again. Which means he'll never get the chance to be cold or thoughtless or hurtful. He will never again be able to sap my energy and make me feel unimportant. I will never have to make everything better for him again.

I didn't really lose very much.

I thought I would get to a place where, after the pain left, I would want to know him again as a friend. We always were good friends. He was just a hideous boyfriend.

What I didn't see coming, though, was that when the pain left, it took everything with it, including any love I felt for him. I don't seem able to recall any happy memories of him. That's never happened to me in a break-up before. No question, this is that one relationship in my life that kicked my ass. I'm glad to have it over and done with.

Is it really possible for me to have that wonderful new man in my life now? Why would such a great guy want me? I'm a mess. A fat, depressed mess.

Can this great guy really see past all of my damage to who I really am on my better days, and fall in love with me?

Where is my faith? Where is my hope? Where is my passion? I can't find any of it.

The first signs of the pain to come all started a year ago, right around now. I've been breaking up for a year!! But not him – he's been gone for good since January, having a lovely new life (or a miserable, suffering life, if the psychic is right – yes please!).

It's just me left here to continue the break-up, pouring out my pain in this journal for heaven knows how much longer.

Please, God, pull me to safety! Get me out of here!

January 19th

Between the last entry and this one I visited the family for the holidays, where things went about as they had last time I was there. No mention of my break-up, no asking how I was doing with it. I suspect they all figured since it had been close to a year, I would be over this completely. Or if I wasn't, then I should be. Mercifully, I wasn't feeling as broken, and was able to get through the holidays with only some twinges of sadness – albeit, some of those twinges were pretty strong, more like charley horses which could really seize me up and leave me breathless.

Being single at the holidays can be a little rough.

Being on your own because you were dumped for another woman and are still trying to patch up your heart is brutal.

So when I got back home, I went to my very wise psychic again and thankfully, she was able to provide me with some more of those same comforting words.

She said that he knows he made a terrible mistake, that he really blew it, and that he made the wrong choice.

Still, that doesn't mean his unhappiness has anything to do with me. He may be miserable with her, but she's not saying he wishes he was with me.

No matter how unhappy he is, he wanted to be with her. As opposed to how he felt about me. He didn't want to be with me, ever. What a complete, world-class fool I was.

But I had a life. It might have had its flaws, but I had a life. How did my life just disappear like that? I suppose I let it happen. I let everything stop, when I was hiding out from the world, trying to pull myself together. I still talked with friends, sometimes saw them – my pride demanded it. I couldn't let them know he had decimated me.

But before the break-up, how could I not see it coming? Could I have stopped it from happening?

People knew me as part of a couple, or at least as being with this man. It was how they – and I – defined me. And then the relationship disappeared. Nothing replaced it. Literally nothing. No new romance on the horizon. Not a buoyant, single-and-loving-it me. Nothing.

There's only a void – a, big, flat, arid emptiness.

Tonight, for the first time in a while, I cried. Because I want my life back.

But it's gone. It's just gone.

February 1st

It's been a year, a whole year, since I last saw him, since I ended it. It's time for the mourning to stop.

What is it that still haunts me after all this time?

I think it's that, not only did he not really love or respect me, he was also ashamed of me. That's been the part I can't get over. I'm not someone to be ashamed of!

He hated for anyone to think we were serious. This is the thing that, all else being equal, will keep me from ever letting him back in my life. I didn't deserve that. He was wrong to feel that way. He was a shit.

I am also haunted by images I get of him going on with his life. Sharing jokes, sharing our recipes, sharing all sorts of intimacies with that woman. His wanting her and not me.

I don't want him back, but how can he just go on, not pausing even for a moment? Nothing about him or his life ever gets out of sorts or out of place?

This is why I need the psychis and her "suffering" insights.

Seven years ago I had the life I'd hoped for, or something close to it, for a few weeks, and then it all went away. So I stayed for six years, looking for more of those happy moments, and having some occasionally, and then I ended up with nothing.

Again, literally nothing. No trace that there was ever a relationship.

My life went down the drain this year, and it's partly my fault. But it's partly his fault to, yet he carries on without missing a step.

I, on the other hand, spent the past year taking to my bed and crying. I cried a lot. I carried around depression like I was mired in quicksand. No comfort anywhere.

And that person who hurt me so terribly, who absolutely broke my heart, doesn't give a shit. He may be unhappy, but he's not leaving her. He's not racing back to me, professing his love. And he never will.

Because Leslie called and told me he changed his status on Facebook to "married".

He never loved me. He took and enjoyed all that I gave, but he never loved me. That's how he could hurt me and never apologize, never look back, never regret.

The worst part is that I can't get past the pain, and there's no answer or special trick to doing so. I'm weary of the pain and I want to pack it up and send it all to him.

But he wouldn't care. He wouldn't take delivery.

He doesn't care that he hurt me. Not one word of apology for lying to me or betraying me or hurting me.

And he had to let me find out through Facebook that he was engaged, and then married. After six years together.

I need him to be an ex-boyfriend, consigned to the past, collecting dust in the attic – or better yet, out of the house and donated to any charity who would have him.

If this was some sort of life lesson I needed to have, it was a doozy. Okay then, please, Universe, let me understand all that I needed to learn from this, and then let me be without the pain.

I'm not okay, God.

I'm in pieces and I'm not getting any better.

Please take this pain from me.

P.S. There is a job in London that I have applied for. I dare not hope, because I definitely don't have the energy to put towards making it happen. It feels impossible, and so far away. But I need to feel like there's at least a ghost of a chance that my life could get better.

Best words I read (I think from the break-up book): My life doesn't have to look like this anymore. Everything, including myself, can change.

February 5th

Why was he so ashamed of me? Just what was so lacking in me, in his eyes? And why couldn't he ever share his good fortune with me? I shared everything I had with him.

How much more do I have to hurt before this is over? How many more times will the painful memories spring back up into my brain?

I was watching a version of "War and Peace" last night, and at the end, Pierre said the most insightful thing:

"When our lives are knocked off course, we imagine everything in them is lost. But it is only the start of something new and good. As long as there is life, there is happiness. There is a great deal, a great deal still yet to come."

Please be right, Pierre.

• • • • • • • • • • • • • •

And here is where the journal ended.

So what happened? Not a word, not even a hint!

Did she go out for cocktails with her girlfriends that night and meet a wonderful new man?

Did she get the job and move to London? Is that when she donated the books with the diary mixed in?

Or did she finally just make it through the pain, and reach that moment where she didn't need the journal anymore?

Whatever happened, did she "make it to safety" before her ex got married?

Oh, please, yes!

Or is it possible that he changed his mind, and tried to win her back?

Oh, please, no!

She just has to be alright, whichever way it went.

I wish I knew who she was, so I could be a friend – or a stranger who she could pour her heart out to. Let her know that I understand every bit of it, even the ugly stuff.

Whatever happened to her, I have to believe it all worked out okay. It always does, eventually. At least that's what I learned… the hard way.

I sat for a while, taking it all in, trying not to be pissed that I didn't get the ending to her story. Then I washed my face, went downstairs and curled up next to Mike, feeling like the luckiest woman in the world.

www.ingramcontent.com/pod-product-compliance
Lightning Source LLC
Chambersburg PA
CBHW071926020426

42331CB00010B/2741